Odds and ends

Priya Mathew

BookLeaf
Publishing

Presentation by *BookLeaf Publishing*

Web: www.bookleafpub.com

E-mail: info@bookleafpub.com

ISBN: 9789357217613

First edition 2023

DEDICATION

To dreamers, thinkers, and inspirers

ACKNOWLEDGEMENT

To everything and everyone who inspired me to write

To Alex, for lending a patient ear and occasional nods of approval

To Joanna, for being my biggest critic and cheerleader

Thank You!

PREFACE

I would describe this book as a collection of short musings inspired by the daily business of life. It depicts a range of sentiments shaped by my life experiences.

As you turn the pages, I hope you will find something that touches your heart and speaks to your soul.

A letter

You weave magic with your words
Infusing breath into a lifeless paper

The stories you tell
Tug at my heartstrings

I catch a glimpse of you
Through the window of my soul

A warm glow tingles my cheeks
Is it love, longing, or just a letter?

Daisies

Sunkissed and swaying
In rhythm with the wind
Blooming where they are planted
Are daisies in a field

Teasing every passerby
With their surreal splendor
Thriving where they are sown
Are daisies in a field

Dainty and demure
Spreading their sweet fragrance
Oh, how delightful
Are daisies in a field

Do you hear me?

As you pack a zillion things into your day
Chasing the clock to meet deadlines
Balancing priorities like a deft trapeze artist
Do you hear me?

Will you pause for a moment?
And take a listen
To me…the tune of your heart!

Will you listen closely?
Will you take heed?
Of a world in those heartbeats waiting to take
flight!

Fireflies

Like fireflies flitting in the dark night
Is it a flicker of hope?
Is it a ray of light?
Or a twinkling of love
That breaks through the murky shadows of the
mind

I must be lucky

The way you look at me
Every time you pass by
I must be lucky

When you smile at me
And it lights up your face like a starlit sky
I must be lucky

Your day starts and ends with me
Yet you never tire of seeing me
What if I'm a mirror on the wall?

I must be lucky!

Laugh lines

The sparkle in your eyes
The warmth of your embrace
The words you speak
Exudes an ethereal charm

Your laughter, wild and free
Echoes in the depths of my soul
Timeless, ageless, you stay

The laugh lines on your face
Surpass all earthly riches
As dazzling diamonds
Solely earned by a life well lived

Memories

I walk down the lane
Lonely and confused
Memories…fresh and green
Carry me back to the bygone days
Soothing my mind like the rush of a crisp
autumn breeze
From lands far away we came
Met under the sun
In a world so new, hand in hand we strove our
way through
Together we laughed and shared our joys
Fought often, yet our bond unbroken
Flickering embers now glow brighter
Kindling the memories of those beautiful days
Then you drifted away with time
Leaving me wondering behind
But memories… stay forever
I cherish them as pearls in the oyster of my heart

Myriad hues

Fascinating fall
Sprightly spring
Wallowing winter
Sunny summer
And their myriad hues
Add a mélange of colours
Painting a pretty picture
In a kaleidoscope
For my eyes to imprint
On the canvas of life

New Year

A New Year
Is it a harbinger of
Happy endings
New beginnings
Fiery Fortitude
Rekindling friendships
Refreshing reconciliations
Mending brokenness
Steely resolutions?

Most of all… is it another chance to
Be yourself
Get it right
And make a fresh start?

Paper boats

Two paper boats raced down the stream
Ferrying their dreams for a brighter tomorrow
Laughing in merriment, they joined the sea
Side by side, they danced with the waves
The waves grew stronger; the sea tossed and
raged

Two paper boats
Trembled and turned
No shore in sight
Nowhere to go

Two paper boats
Emptied their dreams
Into the heart of the sea
Weightless, aimless, empty, and free
Two paper boats
Raced down the sea

Petrichor

The parched land calls out
Yearning for soothing drops of rain
Its barrenness casts a dry spell
Splitting the ground into mosaic-patterned
cracks
When will the wait end?
When will the burning cease?
Hustling wind – do you have an answer?
Passing clouds – do you bring good news?
Thunder rolls at a distance
Heralding hope
Raindrops fall recklessly into the arms of the
waiting land
Petrichor…rises
As the sweet scent of a longing fulfilled

Ripples

The rhythm of ripples
Makes the heart sing
A thousand unsung melodies
Creating a symphony
Transporting us on its musical wings
To a world of dreams and desires
The rhythm of ripples
With its notes in perfect synchrony
Is a masterpiece of the maker
To tune our weary souls

Reminiscence

Etched on the sands of time
Are footprints of reminiscence
Some steady, some faint
Each one tells a quaint story
Walk this cobbled path with me
Laugh with me
Sing with me
Let's make memories
Where our footprints lead us
In the casket of reminiscence

Silent storm

Silent storms roar the loudest
Unleashing their barbed tentacles
A cloud of gloom descends
Heavily on the lap of silence
The laughter that echoed in the hallway
Engulfed now by the eye of the storm
Estranged lovers
Exchange glances
Two stony hearts sway with the storm
Waltzing to the tune of silence

Today

I will choose
Hope over heaviness
Forgiveness over fierceness
Kindness over callousness
Today
I will choose
To be grateful
To let go…
To be free…
Today
Is a gift
A time to heal
Tomorrow is another day
Shaped by the choices I will make today!

Veil

A shroud of mystery
Surrounds your frame
A hermit-like charm defines you
Why are you afraid to peel off the veil?
Set your inner child free
Shine bright, unmasked, and unhindered
Let the treasure-trove of love, you hide within
you
Flow out as the healing balm for a broken world

Wheel of time

The wheel of time is turning
As I stand wondering
Musing…
Time…what are you?
A friend or a foe?
When did the hand that once cradled me turn
into one that needs cradling?
When did the cheerful heart brimming with hope
turn into just a glimmer?
Time, every cog in your wheel tells a story
Some bitter, some sweet, some bittersweet
So, I stand wondering
Time, what are you?
A friend or a foe?

Wings

When…
Did you outgrow my lap?
Did the baby steps become steady strides?
Did the endless babble give way to logical
conversations?
Soon…
You will fly away to chase your dreams
Soaring to heights
Seizing the tailwind
Make…
Your wings stronger, let them carry you farther
Remember, taking time to rest is never a test
Flap them homeward to your loving nest

www.ingramcontent.com/pod-product-compliance
Lightning Source LLC
La Vergne TN
LVHW041301200726
843507LV00014B/3077